Deeply

Dug

In

MARY BURRITT CHRISTIANSEN POETRY SERIES
V. B. Price, Series Editor

Also available in the
UNIVERSITY OF NEW MEXICO PRESS
MARY BURRITT CHRISTIANSEN POETRY SERIES

Miracles of Sainted Earth, Victoria Edwards Tester
Poets of the Non-Existent City,
  Estelle Gershgoren Novak, editor
Amulet Songs: Poems Selected and New,
  Lucile Adler
Selected Poems of Gabriela Mistral,
  edited by Ursula K. Le Guin

A Volume in the Mary Burritt Christiansen Poetry Series

Mary Burritt
Christiansen
Poetry Series

DEEPLY
DUG
IN

R. L. BARTH

UNIVERSITY OF NEW MEXICO PRESS
ALBUQUERQUE

For Susan and Ann

LIBRARY OF CONGRESS CATALOGING-IN-PUBLICATION DATA

Barth, R. L. (Robert L.)
Deeply dug in / R. L. Barth.— 1st ed.
p.   cm. — (Mary Burritt Christiansen poetry series)
ISBN 0-8263-3182-3 (cloth : alk. paper)
1. Vietnamese Conflict, 1961-1975—Poetry.
2. Soldiers' writings, American.
3. War poetry, American. I. Title. II. Series.
PS3552.A7545 D44 2003
811'.54—dc21
2003006712

DESIGN AND COMPOSITION: Mina Yamashita

Contents

Summing Up

I would have rivaled Homer, but the Muse
Gives what she will and writes her own reviews.

Foreword

Political poems, especially about war, are often dismissed as historical artifacts, too ephemeral and specific for universal appeal. This is so even if such poems are clear acts of witnessing with no ideology to pound. But though the poems of R. L. Barth in *Deeply Dug In* are eye-witness accounts by a former U.S. Marine of battlefield conditions in Vietnam, they transcend their moment in history, in much the same way as the ferocity of observation in Goya's etchings, "The Horrors of War," transcend the Napoleonic conflict in Spain.

Barth writes frequently in modern versions of classical Greek and Roman satiric epigrams. But the power of his poems comes not from ancient forms, or from a still agonizing moment in American history, but from the intensity of his presence in situations the mind does not want to remember, his devotion to what is real, and his

steadfastness in fashioning experiences of chaos into poems
in which lucidity allows readers to witness what they
cannot live.

I'm sure some will find these poems difficult to bear
and perhaps will even question why they were written.
Americans, after all, have been told lately that politics
and poetry don't mix well when it comes to ultimate
accolades like White House literary socials. But Barth
replies in almost a low growl to such criticism with a
characteristic directness in a poem introducing a section
called "Small Arms Fire":

Why not adjust? Forget this? Let it be?
Because it's truth. Because it's history.

And in the best tradition of the ancient and honorable
use of invective, he responds in a poem entitled "Don't
You Know Your Poems are Hurtful?":

Yes, ma'am. Like KA-BAR to the gut,
Well-tempered wit should thrust and cut
Before the victim knows what's what;
But sometimes, lest the point be missed,
I give the bloody blade a twist.

Barth's satiric realism takes the epigrammatic poems
of *Deeply Dug In* beyond the sardonic and paradoxical to

ancient metaphors that have the power of war photography.
In a poem called "Reading the *Iliad*," Barth

> Looks upon Greeks and Trojans fighting yet,
> The heroes and foot soldiers, thin and blind,
> Forced-marching for the Styx. . . .

And readers see images of the Bataan death march, of the
Long Walk of the Navajo, of the French marching from
Moscow in the killing winter, of Polish Jews herded into
the showers to be gassed.

Barth never loses himself, or the content of his poems,
in classical allusions and distracting esoterica, even though
he is a translator of the mid-empire Roman poet, Martial,
the master of epigrams. In a poem like "Epilogue," Barth
unwinds the epigram's capacity for piano-wire finality and
concision:

> Twenty years later, the poor sons of bitches
> Learn jungle rot, decaying flesh, still itches
> And, spreading body part by body part,
> Even corrupts the chambers of the heart.

And in "Lessons of War," as in so many other poems,
he moves in for the kill with all the surgical nuance of
Juvenal and his Satires on Roman folly:

Hump extra rounds, frags, canteen, or long ration,
But always shitcan the imagination.

Deeply Dug In is one of those rare and timely books
that connects the present with the past. It brings the reader
to them both in a state of sympathy and understanding.
The reader feels and comprehends that all suffering is the
same. Barth gives us a human place that spans centuries
and allows the common experience of politics and violence
to create a solidarity between ancient Greeks and Romans,
people who've lived through modern wars, and Americans
struggling to regain their equilibrium in a post 9/11 world.
We realize that Homer's lances through the throat, and
Virgil's horror of war, are not just locked away in the icebox
of the past. They usefully describe the present, as Barth's
poems usefully describe not only a common and collective
experience of soldiering and battle, but also the sense that
forced antagonism can become almost reflexive, as the
seventh century B.C. Greek soldier poet Archilochos wrote
in his epigram "Thirst":

I want to fight you
just as when I'm thirsty and want to drink.

Barth's lines in his poem "The Insert" are even more on
the mark:

> We deploy ourselves in a loose perimeter,
> Listening for incoming rockets above
>
> The thump of rotor blades; edgy for contact,
> Junkies of terror impatient to shoot up.

In "Ambush" Barth won't budge from what he saw:

> For thirteen months, death was familiar.
> We knew its methods and the odds. Thus, war.
> And yet, I never once saw dying eyes
> That were not stunned or shattered by surprise.

Why write in the spirit of ancient epigrams? Because it brings strict order, disciplined humor, satire, and concision to the greatest chaos and irrationality humans can experience short of a natural disaster. Virgil described such chaos this way at the end of Book I of the *Georgics*, translated here by Smith Palmer Bovie:

> Unholy Mars bends all to his mad will:
> The world is like a chariot run wild
> That rounds the course unchecked and, gaining speed,
> Sweeps the helpless driver on to his doom.

As a witness, Barth contains, condenses, and displays that madness unrestrained in "Foxhole Theology":

Of all the prayers enticed
    Under the gun,
I've never heard *Sweet Christ,*
    Thy will be done.

Barth speaks across time and space, like an ancient voice at home in a contemporary idiom, using a modern sensibility about universal dilemmas in his poem "A Letter to my Infant Son" written "outside Da Nang." It might as well have been written on the plains of Troy or before the Battle of Actium. He wonders how he will answer his son's eagerness for war stories:

War is not the story
That you would have me tell you, as I heard it.
And what is courage? Too many things, it seems:
Carelessness, fatalism, or an impulse.
Yet it is none of these. True courage is
Hidden in unexpected terms and places:
In performing simple duties day by day;
In sometimes saying "no" when necessary;
In, most of all, refusing to despair.

He tells his son that there are "few glorious stories in this war." That he may

. . .not comprehend the rot,

> Disease, mud, rain; the mangled friend who curses
> The chance that saved him (while you look at him,
> Wishing him dead, almost); the bitterness
> You realize you may not understand;
> The children's bodies, small as yours is now. . .

Barth respects Jimmy Stewart as a story teller over John Wayne, who "embodied the know-nothing or the dupe," because Stewart, bomber pilot,

> . . .knew first hand war's suffering and pain
> And consequently never played a scene
> Perverting combat on a movie screen.

So Barth makes the only choice he can to his son's request, which is the eloquence of silence face to face, and the ordered, constrained truthfulness of art in *Deeply Dug In*.

Perhaps war's most enduring structure is the duality of the grandiose hypocrisy of those who sell it, promote it, and command it compared with the reality of those who do the fighting. As Churchill once said, "Never, never, never believe any war will be smooth and easy, or that anyone who embarks on the strange voyage can measure the tides and hurricanes he will encounter."

Or as Barth has put it in "Allegory for L.B.J.":

So many Isaacs, Abraham!
You needn't even lash
Poor boys to altars; seek no ram;
Just raise your knife and slash.

In a world of conflict like our own, with terrorists and armies moving through the normal world like mythic scenes of carnage, the hard, straight clarity of R. L. Barth's poems of witness serve as a steady guide, mapping reality in a language we can use to help us find our own way out of the minefields of propaganda and the fatal bluster of those who try to lead without knowing the way first hand.

—V. B. Price
ALBUQUERQUE, MARCH 2003

Sometimes in altered forms, these poems have appeared in *Forced-Marching to the Styx*, *Incident at Thanh Phong*, *Looking for Peace*, *Reading the Iliad*, *Simonides in Vietnam and Other Epigrams*, *Small Arms Fire*, and *A Soldier's Time*. The interested reader can find the details of previous periodical and anthology publication in those volumes.

Reading the *Iliad*

Volume and desk, coffee and cigarette
Forgotten, the reader, held in Homer's mind,
Looks upon Greeks and Trojans fighting yet,
The heroes and foot soldiers, thin and blind,

Forced-marching for the Styx. But suddenly
Stunned by the clamor under smoky skies,
Boastings and tauntings, he looks up to see—
Not the god-harried plain where Hector tries

His destiny, not the room; instead, a mountain
Covered with jungle; on one slope, a chateau
With garden, courtyard, a rococo fountain,
And, faces down, hands tied, six bodies in a row.

DEEPLY DUG IN

Go tell the Spartans that we hold this land,

Deeply dug in, obeying their command.

1. Proem

I need *just* war, a people's sense of mission,
And not some general's arrogant ambition
For heroism's context, or my muse's
Tongue-tied except for how that people uses
Not troops, sheep slaughtered, baby-killers, tools,
But, to speak plainly, its unmonied fools.

2. Saigon: 16 vi. 1963

In chaos, judgment took on form and name:
The lotus flared; men burned in your just flame.

3. War Debt

Survive or die, war holds one truth:
Marine, you will not have a youth.

4. Allegory for L. B. J.

So many Isaacs, Abraham!
You needn't even lash
Poor boys to altars; seek no ram;
Just raise your knife and slash.

5. Under Fire

How many, Captain Dawkins, did you send,
Without crowds cheering, to a lonesome end?

6. Initial Confusion

A sergeant barked, "Your ass is Uncle's!" though
It wasn't clear if he meant Sam or Ho.

7. Indoctrination

"First, know the jungle and your enemy;
Learn fieldcraft; use bush discipline; keep this
Firmly in mind: we've kinds of syphilis
Without known treatment—that is, have no truck
With cyclo girls, and then I'll guarantee
That you'll survive your thirteen months. With luck."

8. Bush Discipline

Rigged branch. Chubb lost a hand. With Charlie near
None celebrate till safely in the rear.

9. A Child Accidentally Napalmed

"Why waste your tears on me? Give over grief.
If I knew horror, yet my life was brief."
Some poet will perhaps say that for me.
I'd say, "I suffered an eternity."

10. Terminology

He humps the mountains in monsoon and mist
Who has no woman, is no pantheist.

11. One Way to Carry the Dead

A huge shell thundered; he was vaporized
And, close friends breathing near, internalized.

12. An Old Story

"Hustle the boom-boom girls up here,
But take precautions, hey? I've sent
Back for the rum. We'll drink down fear.
Why should our watch be different?"

13. War Story; or, How Hard Was It?

Monk mumbled the Psalms, even pulling guard,
Until they fragged his ass. It was that hard.

14. What Is Our Life?

A rigged game with the odds not even scanty.
Just play the joker and don't up the ante.

15. Movie Stars

Bob Hope, John Wayne, and Martha Raye
Were dupes who knew no other way;
Jane Fonda, too, whose Hanoi hitch
Epitomized protester kitsch.

16. ARVN Defenders

Go tell the Yanks we died, six apologues:
North Vietnamese gentled running dogs.

17. For Unused Graves

These never died but—was it self-deceit?—
Warred, armed with placards, down an unmined street.

18. Saigon: 30 iv. 1975

We lie here, trampled in the rout;
There was no razor's edge, no doubt.

19. Epitaph

Tell them quite simply that we died
Thirsty, betrayed, and terrified.

20. Up Against the Wall

These dead troops gave their country fame,
Which country travestied their story.
Now, only kin recall each name;
Only the dead recall their glory.

21. Epilogue

Twenty years later, the poor sons of bitches
Learn jungle rot, decaying flesh, still itches
And, spreading body part by body part,
Even corrupts the chambers of the heart.

LOOKING FOR PEACE

We looked for peace, but no good came,

for a time of healing, but behold, terror.

—Jeremiah 8:15

Patrolling silently,
He knows how men will die
In jungles. I am he.
He is not I.

A Letter to the Dead

The outpost trench is deep with mud tonight.
Cold with the mountain winds and two weeks' rain,
I watch the concertina. The starlight-
Scope hums, and rats assault the bunkers again.

You watch with me: Owen, Blunden, Sassoon.
Through sentry duty, everything you meant
Thickens to fear of nights without a moon.
War's war. We are, my friends, no different.

A Letter from an Observation Post: Near An Hoa

Seeming to race the shadow line, eight men
Humped through the thigh-deep paddies—only Hodge
Moving with sureness, shoot by shoot, on point—
Until they neared a tree line. There, he knew,
Hidden within were ruins of a few hooches
Marked as a ville on maps, though long abandoned
By farmers; and by Charlie, during day.

As Hodge was turning to his newest men—
Dragging with six days' hacking mountainsides—
Mortars began to crump, sending them diving
Into the water behind the paddy dikes.
Small-arms fire snapped on both sides, bullets tearing
Through jungle and through mud.

                              Detached by distance
From the fire fight, we watched it like small children
Who have not yet deadened imaginations,
As the shadow line swept village, ridge, and outpost.
Later that night, hearing the sound of choppers,
We saw, gathering darkness to its center,
Their red star cluster die above the trees.

Nightpiece

No moon, no stars, only the leech-black sky,
Until Puff rends the darkness, spewing out
His thin red flames, and then the quick reply
Of blue-green tracers climbing all about.
At night, such lovely ways to kill, to die.

The Insert

Our view of sky, jungle, and fields constricts
Into a sinkhole covered with saw grass

Undulating, soon whipped slant as the chopper
Hovers at four feet. Rapt, boot-deep in slime,

We deploy ourselves in a loose perimeter,
Listening for incoming rockets above

The thump of rotor blades; edgy for contact,
Junkies of terror impatient to shoot up.

Nothing moves, nothing sounds: then, single file,
We move across a streambed toward high ground.

The terror of the insert's quickly over.
Too quickly . . . and more quickly every time . . .

Swift, Silent, Deadly

motto of the 1st Reconnaissance Bn., U.S.M.C.

Somewhere, along the tangled mountain slopes,
Slyly edging the camps and villages,
The tiger pads;
                    he is at once our emblem
And fear and, did he know, almost extinct.

A Letter to My Infant Son

outside Da Nang

Some day, when you are hunting attic trunks
Or hear your buddies boasting of brave fathers,
I know that, all excited, you will ask me
To tell war stories. How shall I answer you?

I still remember my best childhood friends,
Two brothers. How I envied them! Their father
Had given them his medals and his chevrons,
And I remember fumbling with delight
The green and khaki stripes, the tarnished brass.
Happier, sitting still, I heard them tell
Their father's stories, which each night I worked
Through closely, casting and recasting them
In varied forms. Always, I was the hero.

And so, my dear, how shall I answer you?
Shall I be silent when you ask—preferring
Childish amazement, even childish anger,
Trusting you to return with a child's kiss
And quick forgiveness?

War is not the story
That you would have me tell you, as I heard it.

And what is courage? Too many things, it seems:
Carelessness, fatalism, or an impulse.
Yet it is none of these. True courage is
Hidden in unexpected terms and places:
In performing simple duties day by day;
In sometimes saying "no" when necessary;
In, most of all, refusing to despair.
Even suppose a man is brave one time—
Is truly brave, I mean—will he be brave
A second time? In other ways? Perhaps.

There are few glorious stories in this war.
Small child, you will not comprehend the rot,
Disease, mud, rain; the mangled friend who curses
The chance that saved him (while you look at him,
Wishing him dead, almost); the bitterness
You realize you may not understand;
The children's bodies, small as yours is now . . .
War is too much of sentimentality,
Which you soon learn is almost always brutal,
However sad, however pitiful.
So, when you ask some day to hear war stories,
Though I would have you truly understand,
How shall I answer you, if not with silence?

A Letter from the Bush

The triple canopy—
Huge trees, bamboo, and vines—
Constricting sight, we see
All day the jungle designs
Close up: the next vine, leaf,
Branch, or arc of light
Erratic as our grief.
Engrossed, we never sight
Objects that, distant enough,
Permit an azimuth reading.

Nights, we set in—or bluff
The jungle when, proceeding
Noiselessly, each man paces
Himself, fixed on bright wood.
We learn decay that traces
Trails, clearings, even faces
In ambush. It is good.

Outpost Overrun

It was our sixth night. After throwing dice
To set the order of the watch, we slept.
During my watch, the listening-post team slipped
Down the ridge. They only called in twice.

There was no other sound but the faint hum
Of radio handset just inside the bunker.
Across the valley, like a signal blinker,
A fire went out. Nothing but tedium . . .

Next thing I knew, they were inside the wire:
The sappers first, and then a full platoon
Overran posts nobody could maintain.
We shot up flares and opened aimless fire

At everything that moved, trying to fight.
Wounded, I rolled into the garbage dump.
All I remember's my chest turning damp
And someone crying out, "More light! More light!"

A Letter from An Hoc (4), by a Seedbed

Some distance away
you can see, across paddies and woods,
  in this stunned glare of midday,
    six green shades like moods

  that betray the villes
we have been patrolling since first light,
  humping for the far foothills—
    as if in mad flight

  from the privation
of palm-leaf huts, wood hoes, small pieces
  of china, and eyes that shun
    our faceless faces.

  There are no young men:
they are hiding, Viet Cong, or dead.
  Only the old folk, children,
    and empty-breasted

  mothers still remain,
survivors among all their wreckage.
  Are they trying to retain
    some hold? or to edge

from a commitment,
patiently waiting out their desire?
I don't know. Once arrogant,
bringing aid, the fire

of napalm, and lead,
I become one of their witnesses
to history: this seedbed
with its crevices

sluicing through earth's crust;
this seedbed, like a dry pod shaken
over a dead land, like lust
without a woman.

Letter from a Ward

Commandos empty of your manhood, cease
Prowling over this unlit no-man's land
And leave me, if not consolation, peace.
          Go down among the Picts,

Spartans, and Roman Legionaries, hidden
In whirls of brackish vapors: a rowdy band
Boasting of bawdry and of war, wine-sodden,
          Bivouacked along the Styx.

POWs

Lieutenant Gilbert took us down the hill
This morning at first light, sweeping a ville
For sympathizers. I am guarding two:
A hunchbacked mama-san and her child, who
Squat, fingers quick, blindfolded, loosely bound.
It's odd, but neither makes the smallest sound,
Kneading this silence that I cannot fill.

Da Nang Nights
> *liberty song*

The streets are dark and misty,
Until we near the strip
Where bar girls and weak whiskey
Burn the blistered lip.

In sudden light we choose
Lust by lust our bar;
And whatever else we lose,
We also lose the war.

Running in Vietnam

One hundred four degrees: the war's remote
As you dress-right in the P.T. formation,
Although you know the gunny's threat by rote:

"The gooks are all around us!" Aberration?
A mad old lifer's deepest wishful thought?
Eighteen years, two wars, a police action:

He's seen it all, while you have merely fought
In this war, at this time. He orders, "Left face!
Quick time, march!" Your every muscle taut,

You stomp in a jog step, finding a place
In keeping time, as mushrooms of dust fill
Your vision, even as they let him trace

The increased progress winding down the hill.
Six miles to the PX; then the return,
The last five miles a steep grade. Only will

Could push through corrugating heat to earn
Two lukewarm beers, trooper, you will not drink.
The duty tour drags on, and you will learn

The only quick time's running, though you sink
Without a second wind, whatever gunnies think.

Office of the Dead

Death's mostly distant here of late,
And random with the seediness
Of plain bad luck—nothing like Fate.
But the dead are neither more nor less:

Just dead. I check their metal tags
For eight hours, till my duty ceases,
Body-counting the body bags.
I do not have to count the pieces.

Longinus in Vietnam

They command; and I obey,
collecting my combat pay.
Peasant, soldier—it's all one
on this hill where, like passion
seeking an object, I wait
and, watching, I concentrate.
It's truth of a kind, this sense
of sighting down the long lens
at men who scurry to loss,
hung on my spider web cross.

First Watch

The land crawls like a distant ocean
Beneath the mist—there is no sky—
As leeches set the trails in motion.
Night closes. My poncho keeps me dry
Where, huddled on this jagged shelf,
I sit in darkness, sealed in self.

Souvenirs

Da Nang Air Terminal: slouching, small groups
Of shabby short-timers harass the troops
Just disembarked in-country, flaunting flags,
Belt buckles, carbines, gold teeth, and old rags
Of uniforms stripped from the enemy
Or the black market.
                              Everywhere I see
Cunning old salts mount guard on foreign gear,
As if some day they'll need a souvenir
To reassure themselves that they fought here.

Elegy for a Dead Friend

Mock night of black clouds seemingly withdrew
Into deep space; then our break ended too.

Was it the quickened beauty of that day
That made you careless as you forced your way

Beyond the hut's packed earth, through the hedgerows?
Was it that letter? Simply chance? Who knows?

You tripped a mine. Explosion and then scream—
Blast and echo—I heard them in a dream

Of foliage. Dirt fell. Smoke caught my eye
As it drifted across the china sky.

First to reach you, I saw the uniform
Ragged, knee-length; but could not keep you warm

For all my curses, for all my first aid,
Feeling that I, not you, had been betrayed.

You lay there; I, who thought myself long hardened,
Learned fear extended beyond self-regard.

As if that mine was a mirror you confronted,
Face pressed to glass, no matter what I wanted,

You would not slip past, leaving me this loss,
Liking too much your sudden helplessness.

"The Lighter That Never Fails"

Like brambles twisted in a thicket, six huts,
Unmapped, lay squat in jungle on our flank.
We took fire. After mortars and a tank
Cleared the guerrillas, we swept, our rifle butts
At ready, through civilians left to us.
Rice caches and dead buddies—God's grim sign
To His Elect—prompted us when, on line,
We judged the sympathizers, righteous
With Zippos.

             Torching their thatched homes, we built
Altars, then scattered ashes, scattered guilt.

Last Letter

We're haunting these same mountains yet again,
Tracking down phantoms, and my weariness
Soaks in like fear. It deadens even pain.

This afternoon, we found twelve carcasses
Around bomb craters. Though I choked on the smell
Of maggot-breeding flesh at first, I bless

Those bodies now, for they are flaunting hell;
Bless them, for they are shattered and awry;
Bless them, for I have heard the words they tell:

"Come, friend, it is not difficult to die."

Meditations After Battle

I. *Sunt lacrimae rerum. . .*

And all around, the dead! So many dead!
So many ways to die it hurt the heart
To look and feel sun burning overhead.
We stacked the bodies on scorched grass, apart.

II. . . .*et mentem mortalia tangunt*

Death was the context and the only fact.
Amidst the stench, I almost could believe
There was a world of light where, if souls lacked
Broken bodies awhile, they would retrieve
Them, mended; where no one need longer grieve.

Fieldcraft

At last, the senses sharpen. All around,
I listen closely. Under the dull sound
Of distant artillery and the shrieking planes
Diving with napalm; under the dry crack
Of automatic rifles; at the back
Of consciousness, almost, one sound remains:
Mud sucking at bare feet as they are going
Between the rice shoots. Nearly silent. Knowing.

SMALL ARMS FIRE

Why not adjust? Forget this? Let it be?

Because it's truth. Because it's history.

Definition

The epigram is not artillery,
Blockbuster, napalm, mortar, rocketry;
But it is, rather, hunkered deep in mire,
The sniper-scoped guerrilla's small arms fire.

Social Darwinism

Professionally aided,
The Privileged became,
Until the danger faded,
The weak and halt and lame.

For Part of a Generation

Worn out, the toaster, television, car
Are thrown out, junked, or traded for the new
Just as America abandoned you:
Conspicuous consumption, Asian war.

"Don't You Know Your Poems are Hurtful?"

Yes, ma'am. Like KA-BAR to the gut,
Well-tempered wit should thrust and cut
Before the victim knows what's what;
But sometimes, lest the point be missed,
I give the bloody blade a twist.

Grunt Fantasy

Another war and, swabbing tears with sleeves,
Over the coffin a rich mother grieves.

Epitaph for the Fallen at Camerone

after a Latin inscription in les Invalides

Fewer than sixty soldiers lie here, but they fought
An army till submerged in its immensity.
Though life deserted these French troops, honor did not
That 30th day of April, 1863.

"Leaves must be green in spring"

Malvern elms, limbs sap-filled and leaves green,
    Spring an easy consolation;
However, where may they turn, who've known a jungle
    Blasted by defoliation?

Foxhole Theology

Of all the prayers enticed
      Under the gun,
I've never heard *Sweet Christ,*
      Thy will be done.

Martial 8.58

You wear an army surplus coat; it suits you,
  Until some passerby salutes you.

The Rhetorical Tradition

Observe the rites now: politicians
And Legionnaires, all rhetoricians,
Declaiming from the dais glories
They've sucked from war's nostalgic stories.
    Here's what Christ meant when He said,
    "Let the dead bury the dead."

Reading the Op-Ed Page

I missed my generation's test.

Yuppie's nostalgic consonants and vowels
Prove that, though wanting guts, he still has bowels.

Reading a Revisionist History of WWII

Fathers who pandered shameless lies
To ship us out now say we whine
About our plight; they use their powers
Not to redress wrongs but revise
Their history so that, line by line,
It more and more resembles ours.

Tonight you bitch, under too many drinks,
"Fucked over! Got our asses kicked for dinks!"
I leave the obvious alone—in fact,
For wealthy children, to keep theirs intact.

After the War

for Dan Quayle et al.

It's tough to find, however hard one seeks,
Old khaki stripes among the yellow streaks.

Lessons of War

Hump extra rounds, frags, canteen, or long ration,
But always shitcan the imagination.

Down at the VFW

"You catch that little pecker here last night?"
"Him runnin' off about a Gulf *war*, right?"
"Shit, scrappin's more like . . ."
                              "Some guys got no pride..."
"Said that one only counted if you died."

"Kentucky's Money Bonus"

> *Kentuckians who served in Vietnam . . . are entitled to $25*
> *for each month of service, with a maximum bonus of $500.*

Blood money, conscience cash adjusted
To time in-country and they're quit.
What makes me so goddamned disgusted:
Their offer? My accepting it?

Ambush

For thirteen months, death was familiar.
We knew its methods and the odds. Thus, war.
And yet, I never once saw dying eyes
That were not stunned or shattered by surprise.

Epitaph

These conscripts are not dead. You wonder why?
They never lived; only the wealthy die.

Seeing the Wall, Thinking of Clinton

These fifty-seven thousand names—
Depending on one's point of view—
Are severally rebukes, guilts, shames,
Where some are reconciled, it's true,
But no, sir, not the likes of you.

A Little Elegy for Jimmy Stewart

I honor you for this: unlike John Wayne—
"America's embodiment?" Straight scoop:
Embodied the know-nothing or the dupe—
You knew first hand war's suffering and pain
And consequently never played a scene
Perverting combat on a movie screen.

To Sen. Bob Kerrey

You "don't remember it that way." I groan.
You were the hot shot cherry, lost control,
And later used as shield the Free Fire Zone
For body count more execution toll.
Ex-hero, no, this story you would hand on
Is just like you and lacks a leg to stand on.

Epitaph for a Historian

What can the mind achieve? Traveler, see:
Joe Ellis *re*created history.

Debriefing with the General

As memoir I'd entitle it
Scrambled Eggs and Chicken Shit.

To Combat

We've built a wall, incising thirty years
Severally on its enameled face;
And when I view it—no, there are no tears,
No souvenirs and keepsakes laid in place—
I see, beside my shoulder, that cruel grin
Over hammer and chisel crossed, content.
Though we've collaborated, now begin
The new year's work, but without my consent.

*I swore I'd only be a three year cypher
But learn each sweaty midnight I'm a lifer.*

NOTES

This is a small book. It could have been larger, but I prefer to take Martial seriously: "What's the point of writing epigrams if you gather them into a big, fat book?" I would like to thank Gus Blaisdel, Tom D'Evelyn, Beth Hadas, Warren Hope, and Nick Poburko for their interest and belief in these poems. The few notes following are intended merely to prevent the misunderstanding of a handful of references.

Under Fire
Captain Dawkins is Peter Dawkins, famous also as the "lonesome end" for the Army football team. In 1967 the Defense Department issued the film *A Nation Builds Under Fire*. The narrator is John Wayne, who, in one scene, discusses the United States in Vietnam with Dawkins. As the title suggests, the film is a documentary piece of propaganda.

Longinus in Vietnam
The title character is not the philosopher of the sublime but the Roman soldier who, according to tradition, pierced with his spear the side of Christ as He hung on the cross.

To Sen. Bob Kerrey / Epitaph for a Historian
Senator Kerrey can't remember what happened in Vietnam; Pulitzer Prize-winning Mt. Holyoke College history professor Joseph Ellis, who mendaciously claimed Vietnam service before his students for years, remembers what didn't. They are themselves and, unfortunately, types.